SEPARATIONS

Death

By Janine Amos
Illustrated by Gwen Green
Photographs by Angela Hampton

CHERRYTREE BOOKS

A Cherrytree Book

Designed and produced
by A S Publishing

First published 1997
by Cherrytree Press Ltd
327 High St
Slough
Berkshire SL1 1TX

British Library Cataloguing in Publication Data
Amos, Janine
    Death. - (Separations)
    1.Bereavement - Juvenile literature
    I.Title
    155.9'37

ISBN 1 84234 163 4

Printed and bound in Belgium by
Proost International Book Production

CONTENTS

Dear Gran,

I wish you had a phone. I really want to talk to you. Mum says you're coming to stay soon. Please hurry up and come.

I can't believe Dad is dead. I want it to be a lie. He was a good driver. How could he crash into a lorry? Why wasn't he concentrating? The stupid lorry driver must have been going too fast.

Dad promised he was going to teach me to play chess this summer. He can't now. It's not fair. I'll never learn.

I never said Goodbye to Dad that day before he went to work. I was still in bed. He was always on at me to get up on time. Maybe he was cross with me? Maybe that made him crash? I wish I'd said Goodbye. I wish he'd come back.

Everything's whizzing round in my head. Why did it have to happen to my dad?

There are all these people at our house. No one knows what to say. I want them to go away. Mum's got no time for me. I don't want to see my friends. I hate them. I hate myself. I just want to stay in my room. I feel like shouting.

Please come soon.

Love,
Sam

Dear Sam,

I'm writing back straight away. It sounds as if you're really angry at the moment. You're right, it is not fair that your Dad has died. It's awful and terrible, and there's nothing anyone can do to change it. No wonder you feel like shouting. What about bashing a cushion or kicking a football really hard? It might help a bit when you feel really bad.

I'm coming next Tuesday to stay for as long as you and Mum need me. We can talk as much as you like then - or just be together.

Your Dad's crash was an accident, Sam. Nothing you did made it happen. We'll never know exactly what went on. The police said the road was icy and both drivers lost control.

You will learn to play chess, if you want to. We'll put our heads together and think of someone who could teach you.

See you on Tuesday.

All my love

Gran. x x x

5

HANNAH'S BIRTHDAY

It was Hannah's birthday. Today, Hannah would normally bounce out of bed. She would be first up – to collect the post. She would tear open her birthday cards and rush to open her presents.

On this birthday, Hannah didn't feel like getting up at all. She lay in bed with the curtains closed. Hannah's gran had died, just one week ago. Hannah screwed her hands into fists and squeezed her eyes tight shut. "Why did she die before my party?" thought Hannah, angrily. She punched the pillow hard. "Why right now?"

At breakfast, Hannah's mum tried to be cheerful. She was planning the food for the party. "Come on, Hannah," she said, brightly. "Eat up. Then we can pop into town to buy the pizzas."

But Hannah couldn't eat up. "I've got a sore tummy, right in the middle," she said.

Hannah's mum sat down next to her. "I know how much you're missing Gran," she said gently. "But she was very old – she couldn't live for ever."

Hannah banged her fist down on the table. "But I didn't want her to die!" she shouted.

Hannah's mum went to the supermarket on her own. Hannah wandered into the other room. Her dad was there. There were tears running down his face. Hannah felt funny. She'd never seen her dad cry before, not even at the funeral. "I was just thinking about Gran," he murmured.

Hannah put her head down. She twisted her heel into the carpet. "Why did she have to die now?" said Hannah. "I wanted her to be here for my party!"

"She'd be here if she could," Hannah's dad replied. He smiled a little bit. "Your gran loved parties!"

Hannah looked into her dad's face. "She was sad to leave you," he went on, "but she was so tired, Hannah."

Hannah nodded. "I knew that, really," she said. "I know that old people have to die. It's still horrible though, isn't it?"

"Yes," agreed Hannah's dad quietly.

"Mum's gone to get the party food," said Hannah. "She wants me to have a happy birthday."

Her dad looked at her. "It's hard to be happy when you feel sad inside," he said.

They didn't say anything else for ages. Hannah listened to the old clock going Tock, Tock. Then she remembered something. "I haven't opened my present from Gran yet. It's in my room."

"Let's go!" said her dad, holding out his hand.

Hannah's dad sat on her bed. Hannah stood on tiptoe to reach a large parcel down from the shelf.

"Gran said it was something special," explained Hannah. She carefully opened the shiny wrapping paper. Inside was a beautiful party dress of deep blue velvet.

"Oh!" gasped Hannah. "She knew I liked this one – but I didn't think she'd get it for me."

"It looks like Gran wanted you to have a happy birthday, too," said Hannah's dad, smiling.

Dear Aunty Fran,
    Katy's dead and I don't feel sad. I know I should. My own sister has died and I can't cry. When I see Mum and Dad crying I feel so bad. I'm looking forward to things getting back to normal. No more dashing into hospital in the middle of the night. No more tiptoeing around in the afternoon in case we wake Katy up. No more waiting for Katy to die.
    I am scared. I wonder if I'll die soon too. I've got a sore tummy, like Katy had, but Mum and Dad don't listen. My tummy feels worse at night. It's so sore it keeps me awake. That's when I get scared.
    Please write to me soon.
    Lots of love,
    Jude.

        X X X

Dear Jude,
Thanks for writing to me. It's been such a difficult time for you all, no wonder you're hoping things will get better soon. It's natural to feel the way you do. It doesn't mean you didn't love Katy. But it may be a long time before everything does get better.

You're all feeling sad, and when people are so sad their feelings come out in different ways. Your Mum and Dad are crying a lot because they feel so sad (this doesn't mean they don't love you—they do). You sound like you're all mixed up inside. Maybe that's why your tummy is sore? It's your way of being sad.

Do try to tell Mum and Dad how you feel—or could you talk to a teacher you like? If you talk about it, in time the tummy ache will go away.
A big hug.
Aunty Fran.
XXX

13

FEELINGS: WHEN SOMEONE DIES

When someone special dies, it's natural to have all kinds of feelings – some of which you may not understand.

■ People die for all kinds of reasons. Very old people may die because their bodies are tired and worn out. Sometimes young people die too. They get ill and, however much doctors try to help them, nothing makes them better. They die because they are too ill to stay alive. Other people get killed in accidents. Death is the end of life. Once someone is dead, they can never come back to life again.

■ When you hear that someone special has died, you may have lots of different feelings. At times, some feelings will be stronger than others. This can be scary.

■ One feeling may be a very deep sadness. Some children get so sad that it's hard for them to know what the feeling is. They get tummy aches, like Jude, or feel sick.

■ Sam feels angry at his dad for dying and at the lorry driver. Like Sam, you may feel anger at the person who has died – at yourself – at everyone. You may feel really cross with families who haven't had anyone die. It isn't fair.

■ Some children find it hard to believe that the special person really is dead. It's like a bad dream. Others don't feel anything at all. They are numb.

■ All these feelings are natural and they are all OK. A lot of children at this time have many fears and worries. Many children worry that they somehow caused the death of someone they were close to. They wonder if, by thinking or doing something bad, they could have made that person die. Nothing they've said or done has caused that special person to die.

■ When one special person has died, some children fear for the safety of other people in their family. They worry that someone else they love will die suddenly, and don't want to let them out of their sight. Jude worries that she will die now, like her sister.

■ At the time of a death in the family, nothing may seem to make sense any more. You may feel all mixed up. Your parents may be feeling all this too, and that's why it's often hard to help each other. Is there someone else who could come to be with you all at this time?

HOW TO HELP YOURSELF COPE

When someone special dies, it's natural to feel angry, frightened, sad and muddled. There are some ways you can help yourself at this time:

■ Say goodbye to the person you loved and who loved you. Ask to go to the funeral or the special service. If this isn't possible, say goodbye in your own way. Perhaps you could have a quiet time in your room looking at a photograph of the person who has died?

■ Remember that it's not your job to make other people feel better. You can't take the place of anyone who has died either. It's hard enough to take care of yourself when you feel so upset.

■ It might help to find someone – or something, such as a pet – to talk to. Talking won't change what's happened. But it might help to make you feel better.

■ Don't expect to feel better straight away. You'll have good times and bad times – and that's OK. You might feel like doing things you stopped doing ages ago, like taking a bottle to bed with you. It's all right to ask for this.

■ You might like to have a special photograph of the person who has died, just for you. Ask for one.

■ Don't be afraid to ask questions. You might need to know more about the death than you've been told. If your parents find it hard to give you answers, try talking to another adult you trust. If you don't understand, keep asking.

■ Remember that it is still OK to laugh and have fun. Remember, too, that you're not alone. There are a lot of people who care about you.

■ Don't forget, nothing you thought or said caused the special person to die.

Dear Gran,

Guess what? I can play chess. My friend Jason's dad has been teaching us every night after school.

I won a prize for my school for photography. It was in a big competition. You had to take a picture of someone in your family. I took loads of photos of Mum and some of myself. When I got the film developed, the best ones were some old ones I took of Dad in his running gear. It made me feel funny to see them. I'd forgotten they were in the camera. Mum said that a photo of Dad would still count, even though he's dead, so I sent in one of him.

Mrs Franey gave me the prize in front of the whole school. The photo is on my bedroom wall in a big frame. Sometimes it makes me feel sad but I like it being there. It's sort of like my dad is still around.

I went on School Camp last week. I stayed away for two nights but I missed Mum. I told Mr Brook my teacher and we phoned her both days. The next day I wanted to come home. Mr Brook says I can go again next year anyway.

Love from
Sam.

18

Dear Sam,

I did enjoy hearing from you. Well done for learning to play chess and for winning the photography prize. Your Dad would have been very proud of you.

I'd love to have a copy of that photo. Would you be able to get one done for me? It's always nice to have a special photo to help us remember.

Do you remember the first camera he bought you? You were only four and everyone said you were too young to take proper photos. But your Dad loved photography and thought you would too. He was right, wasn't he? You're very like him in lots of ways.

It was good that you got to go on Camp. I bet you're looking forward to next year.

Thinking of you.

Love,

Gran.

xxx

FEELINGS: BETTER OR WORSE?

Even a long time after a special person has died, you may still feel sad and confused. You may also get angry with yourself that you don't feel better. All these feelings are natural.

again. At those times, it's as if the person they loved has only just died.

■ Some children may feel different from their friends and find it hard to join in. They may get angry really easily and shout or try to fight with others. Months or years after the death of the special person, some children still feel scared to be apart from their families. That's why Sam wanted to come home from School Camp. Big

■ Some children find it hard to carry on with everyday life when someone they love has died. They have good days when they can laugh and play. And they also have days when the old, bad feelings come back

changes, like going to a new school or moving house, may feel especially scary too.

■ If your mum or dad has died, in time your living parent may grow to love a new partner. Lots of children find this hard. They worry that this isn't kind to their dead parent. Remember, nothing can take away the love you shared with them. It's yours to keep for ever.

■ It's OK to feel sad, angry and frightened about the death of someone you loved. It's painful too. This pain is called grief and is part of saying goodbye to that person. Take as long as you need.

THE DEATH OF A PET

The first time you learn about death may be when your pet dies. It means you will never see them again. This may feel like the end of the world for you. But it may help to remember that pets and people stay with us in our memories. In this way, they are part of us for ever.

HELPING YOURSELF TO MOVE ON

If you're finding it hard to carry on after someone special has died, there are some things you can do to help yourself:

- Visit a place which makes you think of the dead person. This might be their grave or a place where they liked to be when they were alive. It might be somewhere you had fun together. This can be a special place where you spend time thinking about the person who has died.

- If you have a garden, you could grow a rose or some other plant. It will flower in years to come and help you to remember the person you loved.

- Draw pictures or write about how you feel. Bad feelings can seem less powerful if you put them down on paper. You might want to rip them up afterwards. It's up to you.

■ At times when you're feeling especially upset, it helps to be with someone you know well. If you feel bad, spend some time with someone you trust – until you're feeling good again. It might make you feel better to talk a lot about the person who has died.

■ Even a long time after someone has died, everyone still needs to cry about it sometimes. Remember, it takes time to say goodbye to someone you loved. However long it takes is the right time for you.

DAD'S SPECIAL BOOK

Plop! "There he goes," whispered Richard. Jack looked to where his stepdad was pointing. He just caught sight of the small furry body of a water vole. It slipped into the water and Jack smiled. He was having fun. He liked Richard – he didn't keep talking all the time or asking Jack questions. He showed Jack what to look for and pointed things out. So far they'd seen two water voles and a kingfisher. And they'd shared a whole packet of ginger biscuits.

At four o'clock it was time to pack up. "Race you back to the campsite!" said Richard.

Off they went, scrambling up the steep slope. They reached the top side by side and puffing. Jack's mum was sitting in the sun, reading a book. They flopped down beside her. Richard gently tugged the book away. "Peace is over now," he laughed. "The boys are back!" He held the book up high in one hand.

"I'll get it, Mum!" grinned Jack. He grabbed Richard's legs in a rugby tackle. Soon they were rolling about on the grass, Mum too. Richard was ticklish and he laughed in great, loud chuckles. Jack liked the way his eyes crinkled at the corners. He thought his dad's eyes had been a bit like that.

All at once, Jack pulled away. He got up and dashed inside the tent. Mum and Richard stopped laughing too. He could feel them watching him.

"Hey! What's the matter?" Richard called out.

But Jack couldn't answer him. It was hot inside the tent. Jack kicked off his trainers and lay down on his sleeping bag. He opened his rucksack and pulled out a photograph in a green leather case. He stared hard at the picture of his dad. He'd died three years ago.

Jack closed his eyes and tried to see the face in his mind. He couldn't.

After a while, Jack's mum put her head through the tent flap. "Can I come in?" she asked quietly.

Jack shrugged. His mum crawled in through the opening.

"Remember going camping with Dad?" asked Jack.

"I do," said his mum, smiling. "Remember when Dad put up the new tent and ..."

"It fell down!" finished Jack.

They grinned at each other. "We've got a photograph of that somewhere," Jack's mum went on.

Jack put his head down. "I'm scared I'm forgetting him," he whispered. "I know," answered Jack's mum. "We've got lots of good memories of Dad. Nothing can ever take those away, they're part of our life."

"Do you think Dad would mind us having fun with Richard?" asked Jack slowly.

His mum shook her head. "He wouldn't mind," she said. "Having fun with Richard can't spoil any of the good times we had with Dad."

"Do you know where that tent photo is?" asked Jack.

"Yes," said his mum. "Why don't we make a scrapbook when we get home? Full of all the special things we remember about Dad? We can put that photo in for a start."

Two weeks later, Jack and his mum sat in Jack's room. Balanced on their knees was a fat scrapbook. It was full of pictures, photographs, football programmes and some writing all about Jack's dad. They'd made it together.

Jack patted the book. "It's really big," he said. "I didn't think I remembered so much."

Then Jack saw Richard standing at the door. "Come and see our scrapbook," said Jack.

Richard sat down next to them. Jack slowly turned the pages for him to see. "Wow," said Richard, when they'd reached the end. "You certainly had some fun together, you three."

"We did," said Jack, smiling at him.

Dear Aunty Fran,

Yesterday it was Katy's birthday. She would have been 10 years old. It was really sad. I was crying at school. I didn't go out at playtime. I talked to my teacher about it and I decided to draw Katy a picture as a kind of birthday present. I put in all the things Katy liked best – ice cream, skating, dancing, the Spice Girls, cats, Mum, Dad and me. I put it in Katy's bedroom. It made me feel better. Mum, Dad and I had tea together and we said Happy Birthday, Katy.

I miss her every day and most of all at weekends. We used to do each other's hair and mess around. Last weekend my friend Sophy came to stay. She's got a ponytail. It's good to have someone to play with but she's not the same as Katy.

Lots of love,
Jude.
× × ×

Dear Jude,

It was great to have a letter from you.

I remembered it was Katy's birthday. I spent some time thinking about those dances she showed us. We had great fun, didn't we? Remember when she first taught us to jazz dance? We got our feet tangled up and fell over!

It's great that Sophy stays at your house — I bet you have a lot of fun. Do you want to bring her to stay here when you come?

See you then.

Love,

Aunty Fran. X X

HELPLINES

If you feel really alone, you could telephone or write to one of these offices. Sometimes the telephone lines are busy. If they are, don't give up. Try them again.

ChildLine
Freephone 0800 1111
Address Freepost 1111, London N1 OBR

Cruse Bereavement Line
Telephone 0181 332 7227
or look in the directory for a local number

The Samaritans
Telephone 0345 909090